GEORGE ELIOT

AND

JUDAISM

AN ATTEMPT TO APPRECIATE
'DANIEL DERONDA'

BY

PROFESSOR DAVID KAUFMANN

OF THE JEWISH THEOLOGICAL SEMINARY, BUDA-PESTH

TRANSLATED FROM THE GERMAN

BY

J. W. FERRIER

SECOND EDITION

Printed in the United States of America

GEORGE ELIOT

AND

JUDAISM.

"It is a part of probability that many improbable things
will happen."—ARISTOTLE : *Poetics.*

THERE is a plant in the East, the seeds of
which are lifted by the winds and carried
into every region of the earth. Where
they fall, there they germinate, unaffected
by variations in the nature of the soil,
and proof against any inclemency of at-
mosphere into which they may chance to
have come. The observer stands meditative and amazed at the wondrous power
of growth by which representatives of the

species are enabled to strike root and flourish under the most different climatic conditions.   In spots where the land offers itself kindly and favourably they quickly bud, and attain to a breadth of propagation which narrows the area of the other *flora* of the district, and seems ever to push forward towards sole dominion. As though it were the sun of their home that ripened them, as though the juices of their far-off place of origin ran in them, they advance with prosperous develop- ment till the native growths are seized with fear at these ineradicable children of a foreign soil.   Upon barren cliffs and in lonely abysses — where blossoming and sprouting seem impossible—they know the secret of existence ; they surmount every obstacle, and twine themselves around their unwilling standing-places with insuperable strength, until the ramifications of their fibres, penetrating deeper and deeper into the crags, knit themselves together and strengthen, burst the rocks asunder, and clasp the hard foundations with their mighty arms. They tower aloft in the golden light, as if in insolent disdain of the rugged earth, and soar into the quickening air which breathes around them, heedless whether her blessings be obtained by them as bold, aggressive immigrants, or indigenous, hereditary guests. The ravages of fire and sword, even, cannot permanently outroot them; their stems remain fixed in the ground, protected as it were by some mysterious guardian, and fresh shoots keep ever springing up to renew once more the inherent prolific power of propagation. It is a wild luxuriance of unceasing growth, which does not wait to be tended from without, but finds for itself and draws together the means for its own increase. And for this reason it has maintained its ground without help from the law, which gladly countenances, indeed, all attacks made upon it, and all attempts aimed at its suppression. The globe is overrun with the inevitable plant; what will restrain its unceasing fecundity? Men are almost beginning to abandon themselves helplessly to what cannot be altered, and to study what use there may be in a phenomenon which they cannot get rid of, no matter how well assured they are of its injurious nature.

The comparison may well halt, for it refers to an unique, incomparable existence, the riddle of the history of nations —the Jews. Destroyed as the national independence of Judæa was by Rome, from the bones of the vanquished there had already arisen — the Avenger; a branch severed from the parent trunk became a rod of correction for the oppressor; and a solitary Jewish idea sufficed, in its disfigurement, to shatter the

Roman Mythology and all its faded splendour. And that idea rose to unimagined power, and rolled ever on and on like an avalanche, crushing the states over which it passed. But though it conquered the world, it remained without effect on those who were its originators. Banished from their home, they spread abroad over every land, outwardly disunited, inwardly at one. The Rigid in motion, the Eternal in transition, they advanced through time, deaf to all allurements, hardened against all oppression, and, as it were, insensible. They accepted their destiny as a dark necessity; they did not ask—why? They had a task; they *were forced* to live and to transmit downwards as an inheritance the inviolable legacy left them by the nations. Their path was marked by blood and tears; but faith in the final victory of truth glowed among them; and they believed— they knew—that with them alone did the

truth abide.   Thus, harassed by all, they
have survived all; and when the dawn of
a happier age began to break for them as
for others, it illuminated a people numeri-
cally greater after eighteen hundred years
of oppression and persecution than in the
days of its highest power, and a race able
to enrich every literature of the world
from its treasures, even after men had in-
humanly and treacherously sought to deprive its mental life of light and air.   Use
and wont are the hereditary enemies of
every novel and striking phenomenon; and
it has long since been pointed out that the
workings of Nature make small claim upon
our admiration, only because we have been
accustomed to move among them from our
cradles.   In this way the world has come
to regard the Jews as a matter of course,
and has grown dull to the miracle which a
contemplation of their existence reveals—
which is humorously expressed by Heine

when he says that we must go many thousand miles indeed to see *one* Jew, too
many of them in the world though there
be. This dulness is not universal, however; and a gush of devotion, a feeling
of meditative surprise, occasionally comes
over an unbiassed mind when it succeeds
in vividly realising the fact that the Jewish
race still exists, and when it reflects what a
vast output of heroic strength and joyous
martyrdom must have gone before in order
to render that fact a possibility.

It is more, however, by the question of
the future of the Jews than by the enigma
of their marvellous preservation that public reflection is demanded. Is the end
and result of their glorious history to be
their fusion and disappearance among the
nations of the earth? Why then all this
loving care? why these grievous chains?
why these streams of blood and tears?
Is this despised minority, from whose

womb have sprung the religions which
rule mankind, still to be called upon, at
the grave of her daughters, to comfort and
lift up a despairing world? Or will the
semblance of unity which even now, if in-
visibly, binds together her dismembered
limbs, grow paler and paler in the sunlight
of progress? Will the hopes with which
the thirsty have for centuries allayed their
pangs keep ever running drier and drier,
and finally shrink to the miserable rem-
nant to which they are compared by shallow merriment? Are the Jews still a
people, a sickly body indeed, but one to
which youth and health may return, or a
bleached and scattered heap of bones?
Are these bones destined ever again to
live and move? The questions which
arise in the contemplative mind at the
spectacle of the Jewish community are not
easy to answer.

And what are the opinions of the Jews

themselves on this point? It is the sign of a sound organism that its members perform their functions unconscious of activity. No charge, therefore, can be brought against the Jews when the assertion is put forward that, as yet, they have adhered to their doctrines with absolute and unwavering fidelity, but *without a definite consciousness of their national vocation.* They have defended a trust, the future of which is raised and established in their eyes beyond all doubt, without subtilising concerning its peculiarities. Judaism has, certainly, at all times been more than a mere religion for its adherents. It has been for them not only a means of satisfying transcendental desires and a theory of their relations with heaven, but also their rallying-point in dispersion and the necessary condition of their existence as a state, shattered, indeed, but secretly living on in exile. Alongside of their

attachment to the ancient land of their
birth, the sentiment of a long-lost home
lay in their hearts, towards which they
were drawn by peaceful longing expressed
in heartfelt songs and prayers, not in re-
bellious or perfidious efforts for freedom,
—in wishes and in hopes, not in deeds
and strivings.   Fusion with the nations
of the earth was forbidden them, even had
the laws of those nations permitted it;
and therefore they have brought their
old facial traits down to posterity along
with the teachings of their forefathers.

In this inquiry we must not overlook
the fact that it is only in this century that
the idea of Nationality has reappeared in
all its antique sharpness of outline; and
that, so late as the end of last century,
it was regarded as the highest achievement of culture to have triumphed over
national narrowness by presaging Universal Humanity.   Mediævalism, which in the

old world reaches further down than the
era of the French Revolution, was not
national, in our sense; and therefore that
cannot be demanded from the Jews which
was wholly lacking to their circumstances.
It has been reserved first for Hate and
then for Science to begin, in this century,
the recognition of a nationality among the
Jews. For if attention has always been
directed to the fact that evidences of
Jewish descent follow deserters from their
colours even to the fourth degree, in spite
of all the paint of mock-enlightenment and
the holy water of conversion, as though
avenging Nature insisted upon retaining
the hateful hereditary blemish in the features of the renegade; so it more espe-
cially challenged reflection at a time when
investigation aimed at going to the roots
of phenomena, and progress made bold
to demand rights for the long-oppressed
aliens. On one side enemies were work-

ing unceasingly to advance new arguments which should prove the Jews to be a peculiar people, never amalgamating with their fellow-citizens; on the other side Science was bringing to light infallible marks by which the physical peculiarity of the Jewish race should be made clearly manifest.

With the alteration in the views of Judaism entertained by the outside world, the change which came over the aspects of this question among the Jews themselves advanced *pari passu.* Mendelssohn, indeed, partly on account of his singular want of historical knowledge, and partly on account of his dread of arousing watchful hatred, saw himself forced to deny that his race were the inheritors of a separate Nationality. Newly awakened though it doubtless was, the pulpit oratory of the Jews at the beginning of this century is so colourless, and bears such small trace of a national stamp, that we are compelled in perusing it to regard Judaism as a pale creed akin to the other religions of the world, and as a bloodless figment of the mind, rather than as a great spiritual power, and a rapturous conception of the universe throbbing in the breasts of its adherents, and making lions out of lambs. But it may be boldy maintained that *the Judaism of to-day is awakening to, and strengthening in, national self-consciousness.* The history of German pulpit eloquence among the Jews will have to take note of this phenomenon and portray its growth; and a comparative glance at the works of *Jost* and *Graetz* shows us what measure of significance the national movement has attained to in modern thought. The consciousness of the wonderful union of Religion and Nationality in Judaism has already become so distinct that men are beginning to sever the inseparable, and to declare themselves enthusiastic admirers of its national, while they have long since cast away its religious side, as an irksome chain. I see a signal voucher for this change in the use of the word " Jew:" it is now no longer shunned by the Jews themselves; whereas, formerly, they were timidly and shamefacedly wont to substitute for it " Israelite," and various similar terms. No one will maintain that faith has soared to any very great elevation among the Jews, in recent decades; nevertheless, in comparison with earlier times, figures prove that apostasy has become rare among them. The reason usually alleged is, that their increasing liberty and ameliorated condition render that step superfluous; but fully to explain the fact, it must be noted that the Jews themselves have begun to recognise a *nationality* in Judaism—and a nationality which cannot be laid aside like a garment.

What will follow this awakening? Will that force inherent in the idea of nationality, which leads to the formation of States, and which, in recent times, has so wonderfully transformed the map of Europe, impel the Jews also to be in earnest with the hopes of thousands of years, and turn their patient longings into rapid actions? Will the march of history lead them, after all their wanderings and sufferings, to re-establish a definite centre, and solemnly to complete their outward and visible unification? On this point the Jews are divided into two camps. For the one party the hope of rebuilding the ancient State is a childish and ridiculous enthusiast's dream, and the desire for a return to Sion an empty lie, for the obliteration of which from all forms of prayer moral duty calls, if truthfulness before the Almighty is to be respected; for the other party these longings are as the

breath of Jewish national life, and their
expression is a sacred command, and an
inviolable law.   In spite of all blustering
and quarrelling, however, the fact cannot
be denied that, for the *greater* portion of
the Jews, Palestine is something more
than a mere geographical notion; and
that all the weaning of centuries, and all
the enlightenment of modern times, have
been unable to banish a longing for that
land from their hearts, or to destroy the
memory of it in their thoughts.   Advanced culture and noble magnanimity are
not yet too tired to prove by deeds their
readiness to sacrifice themselves for that
country and its inhabitants, and to step
forward for the preservation of places
upon which the adoration of three religions, but above all the heart and soul of
Judaism, is fixed.   Who will venture to
predict what may one day be brought
about by the flood-tide swelling in the

Jewish race? Who will venture to maintain that the imponderable mass of indefinite forebodings and mysterious impulses, which has increased rather than diminished in the soul of Judaism while the centuries have run their course, will vanish into air without having achieved result?

The events of universal history are not to be reckoned upon either by the short-sightedness of the Philistine or by the narrow-sightedness of the student. When the hour was ripe the Augustine monk became the father of the Reformation. The death of Islamism had been already proclaimed, when the Wahabees burst forth from their mountain fastnesses and flamed through Arabia with a religious fervour unknown in modern times — a warning and a lesson to men not to class even Mohammedanism with the things of the past. Has not the Sick Man be-

come proverbial ? Have not political star-
gazers foretold the very moment of his last
death-rattle ? A statesman like Midhat
Pasha shows the world what sort of forces
can be set in motion by a State tottering
on the very verge of ruin. And Jewish
history itself ? The nine times Wise of the
Babylonian Captivity smiled contemptu-
ously at the fire of the prophets, and looked
down with pity on the miserable creatures
whose crazy infatuation it was to rebuild
the temple ; but from the midst of these
very sufferers there arose minds to herald
a new epoch for Judah, and to bring im-
mortality to Judaism. And even when
the race again lay broken on the ground,
borne down with meek submissiveness
beneath the Roman yoke, there blazed
forth Bar-Cochba, the Son of the Star, and
hosts of devoted warriors sprang from the
earth, compelling Rome to send her ablest
commander to coerce them, a handful

though they were. Nor did the inhuman
lord of oppression set his iron heel upon
the backs of the vanquished till streams
of the blood of Judah's heroes had flowed
down to the Mediterranean, and till
treachery had crept in and broken their
serried ranks. The defenders of Jerusa-
lem and the heroes of Bethar did not
surely bleed in vain! From the leonine
uprising of Judæa, and from the safe and
wondrous return of the exiles from the
Babylonian Captivity, should not the lesson for all time be drawn that the deep-
rooted love and longing of the Jewish
people for Palestine is something more
than a wild and antiquated absurdity,
something more than a barren dream of
foolish enthusiasm? Feelings and sentiments which are worthy to be cherished
and preserved in a nation's soul against
all the influences of time are wont to con-
centrate themselves in great personalities,

and to impart to them a power of attrac-
tion, before which moderation and half-
heartedness fly like leaves before the storm.
The history of Israel presents a number
of such figures.   Ezra and Nehemiah succeed to the Prophets of the Captivity,
John of Giskala stands beside Judas Mac-
cabæus, Akiba - ben - Joseph defends the
Star-Son of Bethar, and even through the
darkness of the Middle Ages the fiery
pillar of Jehuda-ha-Levi gleams forth.
Shall we some day be able to say—" and
so on " ?

It is to an English Christian authoress
that the historian of culture must assign
the glory of having grasped these ideas
most profoundly, and of having perceived
with the prophetic eye of genius the
proper moment for answering the fundamental questions of Judaism, and investing
them with a poetic charm.   Much can be
adduced to explain this circumstance —

nothing to weaken it. It can be pointed out that it is in England pre-eminently that the Jews have the courage to confess their nationality, and to bring it into bold relief. Nor have they cause, nowadays, to fear vexatious interference with their rights on that account : the English are too mature in wisdom not to allow true citizens their harmless hopes ; knowing as they do from their own experience that men can give all due allegiance to a foreign State without ceasing to belong to their own people. English literature, too, is by no means poor in authors tolerant and well-disposed towards the Jews. It is now a matter of almost perfect scientific certainty that Shakespeare was far from drawing a mere caricature in Shylock ; and the " Merchant of Venice," rightly regarded, must be taken as giving most powerful evidence of the independence of judgment and deep sense of justice which

led the prince of poets to become the
advocate of the down-trodden race. And
let us not forget the loving hand with
which Walter Scott has drawn the character of Rebecca, the Jewess, in 'Ivanhoe.'
Hebrew annals proudly record that shin-
ing foremost in the ranks of those who
fought for Jewish emancipation was the
king of English historians, Thomas Bab-
ington Macaulay. Dickens, even, who
did not always wish well to the Jews, has
graced his novel, 'Our Mutual Friend,'
with the ideal picture of Riah. Is it necessary to speak of the glowing enthusiasm
with which no less a man than Benjamin
Disraeli has glorified the race in many of
his works — the same Disraeli who, as
Lord Beaconsfield and Prime Minister of
the English Crown, shows himself, in hon-
ourable contrast with many men of commoner stamp, proud of the Jewish blood
running in his veins? These facts tell

much in England's honour; but even in
her literature there are not wanting voices
to calumniate the Jews and Judaism; for
it is exactly because in her midst the
Jewish people have public justice accord-
ed them in their quality of Jews that the
Jew passes all the more for an alien, and
must, in consequence, bear the weight of
prejudice, like everything unknown. Thus,
all instances taken together of just and
magnanimous treatment received by the
Jews in England up to this time, can
detract but little from the importance of
the fact that the most celebrated authoress
of the day, and the pride of English let-
ters—George Eliot—has chosen Judaism
and its future as the theme of her latest
imaginative creation, with a depth of comprehension hitherto unreached, and with
unexampled grandeur and independence
of judgment. In the Valhalla of the Jewish people, among the tokens of homage

which the genius of centuries has offered
and laid down, 'DANIEL DERONDA' will
take its place as the proudest testimony
of English recognition.

It may be boldly maintained without
fear of exaggeration that no great work
of any modern literature not written by a
Jew has taken Judaism so specially for its
subject as this latest creation of the English authoress; and if it were not that
every mental product is by nature unfet-
tered and essentially opposed to restric-
tion within narrow limits, I would not
hesitate to propose as the formula of this
work, expressing its entire significance,
and all its tendencies, *the Future of Judaism, and its influence upon its adherents.* Lessing has already pointed out, in
a memorable passage, that poetry, in all
cases where it aims at representing a sen-
suous image or event, must confine itself
strictly to portraying the effects which can

be referred to the object depicted. A likeness can never be produced by a bare enumeration of the individual features of a human face; and, in the same way, the poet who can only say what a thing *is*, and not what *its effects* are, and how it reveals itself by impression on the senses, labours in vain, however great and however delicate may be his expenditure of observation. Now we can expand this fundamental axiom of the poetic art, and apply it to the poetic treatment of intellectual forces and phenomena, which must not be delineated in a disjointed and fragmentary manner, but must, on the contrary, appear before us as influences affecting mankind, and find their expression in characteristic motives. It was not to be expected, therefore, from a genius such as George Eliot, that she would present us, in her work, with a text-book of Judaism, with an exposition of her own preferences, or with a critical comparison between it and other religious systems. She does not introduce us to ideas, but to men and women of flesh and blood in whom these ideas work and act consciously and unconsciously; we are shown not a creed, but its professors—not a faith, but those who have been nurtured in it. None but a poetess cunning to transform *convictions into motives, and thoughts into actions,* would have ventured to animate her work with a sentiment so strange and even unintelligible to the majority of the cultivated as the longing of the Jews for the re - establishment of their kingdom. In contemplating a work of art, it is not a matter of *primary* inquiry whether an idea be true or false, whether a sentiment be authorised or not; we have only to consider whether or not the work has succeeded in adequately representing the power of that idea or the dominion of that

sentiment. George Eliot has taken care
to draw her figures true; and no sym-
pathetic reader can gainsay her there, that
even this much - ridiculed longing after
Palestine is well fitted to inform a human
life with rapturous and noble impulses.
This ardent desire for a national future
on the part of the Israelites forms the
intellectual centre and heart of her book.
She has expressed herself on this point
with all desirable clearness; and as it
would be presumptuous to attempt to
put in other words what she has so in-
imitably given utterance to herself, her
ideas concerning the future of the Jewish
nation may be quoted here as they stand
in her work :—

"The life of a people grows, it is knit together
and yet expanded, in joy and sorrow, in thought
and action ; it absorbs the thought of other
nations into its own forms, and gives back the
thought as new wealth to the world ; it is a

power and an organ in the great body of the nations. But there may come a check, an arrest ; memories may be stifled, and love may be faint for the lack of them ; or memories may shrink into withered relics—the soul of a people, whereby they know themselves to be one, may seem to be dying for want of common action. But who shall say, ' The fountain of their life is dried up, they shall for ever cease to be a nation'? Who shall say it ?   Not he who feels the life of his people stirring within his own.   Shall he say, ' That way events are wending, I will not resist'? His very soul is resistance, and is as a seed of fire that may enkindle the souls of multitudes, and make a new pathway for events. . . .

"But what is it to be rational—what is it to feel the light of the divine reason growing stronger within and without ?   It is to see more and more of the hidden bonds that bind and consecrate change as a dependent growth—yea, consecrate it with kinship: the past becomes my parent, and the future stretches towards me the appealing arms of children.   Is it rational to drain away the sap of special kindred that makes the families of man rich in interchanged wealth, and various as the forests are various with the glory of the

cedar and the palm? When it is rational to say,
'I know not my father or my mother, let my
children be aliens to me, that no prayer of mine
may touch them,' then it will be rational for the
Jew to say, 'I will seek to know no difference
between me and the Gentile, I will not cherish
the prophetic consciousness of our nationality
—let the Hebrew cease to be, and let all his
memorials be antiquarian trifles, dead as the
wall-paintings of a conjectured race. Yet let
his child learn by rote the speech of the Greek,
where he adjures his fellow-citizens by the bra-
very of those who fought foremost at Marathon
—let him learn to say, that was noble in the
Greek, that is the spirit of an immortal nation!
But the Jew has no memories that bind him to
action ; let him laugh that his nation is degraded
from a nation ; let him hold the monuments of
his law which carried within its frame the breath
of social justice, of charity, and of household
sanctities—let him hold the energy of the prophets, the patient care of the Masters, the forti-
tude of martyred generations, as mere stuff for
a professorship. The business of the Jew in all
things is to be even as the rich Gentile.' . . .
 " Each nation has its own work, and is a mem-

ber of the world, enriched by the work of each.
But it is true, as Jehuda-ha-Levi first said, that
Israel is the heart of mankind, if we mean by
heart the core of affection which binds a race
and its families in dutiful love, and the reverence for the human body which lifts the needs
of our animal life into religion, and the tenderness which is merciful to the poor and weak
and to the dumb creature that wears the yoke
for us.   .   .   .

"Let their history be known and examined;
let the seed be sifted, let its beginning be traced
to the weed of the wilderness—the more glorious will be the energy that transformed it.
Where else is there a nation of whom it may be
as truly said that their religion and law and moral life mingled as the stream of blood in the
heart and made one growth—where else a people
who kept and enlarged their spiritual store at the
very time when they were hunted with a hatred
as fierce as the forest-fires that chase the wild
beast from his covert?   There is a fable of the
Roman, that swimming to save his life he held
the roll of his writings between his teeth and
saved them from the waters.   But how much
more than that is true of our race?   They

struggled to keep their place among the nations
like heroes—yea, when the hand was hacked off,
they clung with the teeth; but when the plough
and the harrow had passed over the last visible
signs of their national covenant, and the fruitful-
ness of their land was stifled with the blood of
the sowers and planters, they said, 'The spirit
is alive, let us make it a lasting habitation—lasting because movable—so that it may be carried from generation to generation, and our sons
unborn may be rich in the things that have
been, and possess a hope built on an unchange-
able foundation.' They said it and they wrought
it, though often breathing with scant life, as in a
coffin, or as lying wounded amid a heap of slain.
Hooted and scared like the unowned dog, the
Hebrew made himself envied for his wealth and
wisdom, and was bled of them to fill the bath of
Gentile luxury; he absorbed knowledge, he dif-
fused it; his dispersed race was a new Phœnicia
working the mines of Greece and carrying their
products to the world. The native spirit of our
tradition was not to stand still, but to use re-
cords as a seed, and draw out the compressed
virtues of law and prophecy; and while the
Gentile, who had said, 'What is yours is ours,

and no longer yours,' was reading the letter of
our law as a dark inscription, or was turning its
parchments into shoe-soles for an army rabid
with lust and cruelty, our Masters were still
enlarging and illuminating with fresh-fed interpretation. . . . But the dispersion was wide,
the yoke of oppression was a spiked torture as
well as a load ; the exile was forced afar among
brutish people, where the consciousness of his
race was no clearer to him than the light of
the sun to our fathers in the Roman persecution, who had their hiding-place in a cave, and
knew not that it was day save by the dimmer
burning of their candles. What wonder that
multitudes of our people are ignorant, narrow,
superstitious ? . . .

" What wonder ?   The night is unto them,
that they have no vision ; in their darkness they
are unable to divine ; the sun is gone down
over the prophets, and the day is dark above
them ; their observances are as nameless relics.
But which among the chief of the Gentile
nations has not an ignorant multitude ? They
scorn our people's ignorant observance ; but the
most accursed ignorance is that which has no
observance—sunk to the cunning greed of the

fox, to which all law is no more than a trap or
the cry of the worrying hound. There is a degradation deep down below the memory that
has withered into superstition. In the multitudes of the ignorant on three continents who
observe our rites and make the confession of
the divine Unity, the soul of Judaism is not
dead. Revive the organic centre : let the unity
of Israel which has made the growth and form
of its religion be an outward reality. Looking
towards a land and a polity, our dispersed
people in all the ends of the earth may share
the dignity of a national life which has a voice
among the peoples of the East and the West—
which will plant the wisdom and skill of our
race so that it may be, as of old, a medium of
transmission and understanding. Let that come
to pass, and the living warmth will spread to
the weak extremities of Israel, and superstition will vanish, not in the lawlessness of the
renegade, but in the illumination of great
facts which widen feeling, and make all knowledge alive as the young offspring of beloved
memories. . . .

"I praise no superstition, I praise the living
fountains of enlarging belief. What is growth,

completion, development? You began with
that question, I apply it to the history of our
people. I say that the effect of our separateness will not be completed and have its highest
transformation unless our race takes on again
the character of a nationality. That is the
fulfilment of the religious trust that moulded
them into a people, whose life has made half
the inspiration of the world. What is it to
me that the ten tribes are lost untraceably,
or that multitudes of the children of Judah
have mixed themselves with the Gentile populations as a river with rivers? Behold our people
still! Their skirts spread afar; they are torn
and soiled and trodden on; but there is a jew-
elled breastplate. Let the wealthy men, the
monarchs of commerce, the learned in all knowledge, the skilful in all arts, the speakers, the
political counsellors, who carry in their veins
the Hebrew blood which has maintained its
vigour in all climates, and the pliancy of the
Hebrew genius for which difficulty means new
device—let them say, 'we will lift up a stand-
ard, we will unite in a labour hard but glorious
like that of Moses and Ezra, a labour which
shall be a worthy fruit of the long anguish

whereby our fathers maintained their separateness, refusing the ease of falsehood.' They
have wealth enough to redeem the soil from de-
bauched and paupered conquerors; they have
the skill of the statesman to devise, the tongue
of the orator to persuade. And is there no
prophet or poet among us to make the ears
of Christian Europe tingle with shame at the
hideous obloquy of Christian strife which the
Turk gazes at as at the fighting of beasts to
which he has lent an arena? There is store of
wisdom among us to found a new Jewish polity,
grand, simple, just, like the old — a republic
where there is equality of protection, an equality which shone like a star on the forehead of
our ancient community, and gave it more than
the brightness of Western freedom amid the des-
potisms of the East. Then our race shall have
an organic centre, a heart and brain to watch
and guide and execute; the outraged Jew shall
have a defence in the court of nations, as the outraged Englishman or American. And the world
will gain as Israel gains. For there will be a community in the van of the East which carries the
culture and the sympathies of every great nation
in its bosom; there will be a land set for a halt-

ing-place of enmities, a neutral ground for the East as Belgium is for the West. Difficulties? I know there are difficulties. But let the spirit of sublime achievement move in the great among our people, and the work will begin. . . .

"What is needed is the leaven—what is needed is the seed of fire. The heritage of Israel is beating in the pulses of millions; it lives in their veins as a power without understanding, like the morning exultation of herds; it is the inborn half of memory, moving as in a dream among writings on the walls, which it sees dimly but cannot divide into speech. Let the torch of visible community be lit! Let the reason of Israel disclose itself in a great outward deed, and let there be another great migration, another choosing of Israel to be a nationality whose members may still stretch to the ends of the earth, even as the sons of England and Germany, whom enterprise carries afar, but who still have a national hearth and a tribunal of national opinion. Will any say 'It cannot be'? Baruch Spinoza had not a faithful Jewish heart, though he had sucked the life of his intellect at the breasts of Jewish tradition. He laid bare his father's nakedness and said, 'They who scorn him have the higher wisdom.' Yet Baruch Spinoza confessed, he saw not why Israel should not again be a chosen nation. Who says that the history and literature cf our race are dead ? Are they not as living as the history and literature of Greece and Rome, which have inspired revolutions, enkindled the thought of Europe, and made the unrighteous powers tremble ? These were an inheritance dug from the tomb. Ours is an inheritance that has never ceased to quiver in millions of human frames. . . .

" The spirit of our religious life, which is one with our national life, is not hatred of aught but wrong. The Masters have said, an offence against man is worse than an offence against God. But what wonder if there is hatred in the breasts of Jews, who are children of the ignorant and oppressed—what wonder, since there is hatred in the breasts of Christians ? Our national life was a growing light. Let the central fire be kindled again, and the light will reach afar. The degraded and scorned of our race will learn to think of their sacred land, not as a place for saintly beggary to await death in loathsome idleness, but as a republic where the Jewish spirit manifests itself in a new order founded on the old, purified, enriched by the experience our greatest sons have gathered from the life of the ages. How long is it?—only two centuries since a vessel carried over the ocean the beginning of the great North American nation. The people grew like meeting waters—they were various in habit and sect—there came a time, a century ago, when they needed a polity, and there were heroes of peace among them. What had they to form a polity with but memories of Europe, corrected by the vision of a better? Let our wise and wealthy show themselves heroes. They have the memories of the East and West, and they have the full vision of a better. A new Persia with a purified religion magnified itself in art and wisdom. So will a new Judea, poised between East and West—a covenant of reconciliation. Will any say, the prophetic vision of your race has been hopelessly mixed with folly and bigotry; the angel of progress has no message for Judaism—it is a half-buried city for the paid workers to lay open—the waters are rushing by it as a forsaken field? I say that the strongest principle of growth lies in human choice. The sons of

Judah have to choose that God may again choose them. The Messianic time is the time when Israel shall will the planting of the national ensign. The Nile overflowed and rushed onward : the Egyptian could not choose the overflow, but he chose to work and make channels for the fructifying waters, and Egypt became the land of corn. Shall man, whose soul is set in the royalty of discernment and resolve, deny his rank and say, I am an onlooker, ask no choice or purpose of me? That is the blasphemy of this time. The divine principle of our race is action, choice, resolved memory. Let us contradict the blasphemy, and help to will our own better future and the better future of the world—not renounce our higher gift and say, ' Let us be as if we were not among the populations;' but choose our full heritage, claim the brotherhood of our nation, and carry into it a new brotherhood with the nations of the Gentiles. The vision is there; it will be fulfilled."

In these words which the authoress puts in the mouth of Mordecai, the Precursor of him who is to fulfil them, we

have the utterances not only of the
speaker's soul, but of the very soul of
poetry. The accuracy, too, with which
these ideas are expressed deserves our
highest admiration, and our wonder is
elicited in equal measure by their depth
and by their lucidity; a warm heart and a
clear head have united to elaborate them.
We have to note, in this impressive picture, one of the highest triumphs of crea-
tive imagination; for the authoress has
succeeded in bringing before us, in all its
inward, compelling power, and in all its
fiery, action-craving impetuosity, no common passion of mankind, well known
and easy to understand, but a special
sentiment shared by few, strange, and
therefore incomprehensible to the many.
We have here another confirmation of
the saying that the poet is "*von allem
Dasein, das Wesen selbst*" of what he
represents, and another proof that he has,

to use an expression of George Eliot's
own, like the hundred - gated Thebes,
manifold openings to his soul by which
events and phenomena of life, unseen and
unheard by his dull fellow-creatures, gain
access to him. That this book presents
Judaism as the seed of fire and as a
motive power, be it among a mere handful on the earth, constitutes not only its
poetical truth and beauty, but also its
poetical justice; and herein, too, lies the
peculiarity which distinguishes George
Eliot's treatment of the Jews from the
traditional misusage to which other authors have been wont to subject them.
It is not the custom of great imaginative
writers to fling out the traits of their
dramatis personæ like worthless counters,
but to present so many only as are ab-
solutely necessary for the explanation of
the Inward by the Outward, and exactly
sufficient to bring before us the image of

the characters represented; and, therefore,
when we find Judaism beneath these traits,
we are justified in assuming that it has
been introduced for the purpose of explaining the peculiarities inherent in those
who bear them. If these peculiarities are
hateful and mean, the reader will form
an idea that it is the writer's aim to
bring out the vices and moral defects
of Judaism; and, in this way, every caricature which is drawn of a Jew serves
to increase the slumbering and lurking
animosity with which the race is regarded.
But if, as is generally the case, these sins
and shortcomings have no real connection
with Judaism, in spite of their being
notched on her tally, then the writer has
degraded himself, and has become a pan-
der to profligacy, an instigator of low
passion, a calumniator, and a liar; and he
who has no more to say about the Jews
than that they have hooked noses and

a corrupt speech, or that their lives are
spent in usury and sordid avarice, cannot
escape the reproach of the baldest crude-
ness by any degree of poetical varnish.
In a country which can lay claim to the
honour of having brought its hatred of
the Jews to the position of a true science,
and in whose earlier literature, as has been
shown by Zunz from Grimm's '*Wörter-
buch*' * "the quotations vouching for antiquated and obsolete words, when they
relate to Jews, invariably express ridicule
and contempt," — in such a country it
could not fail that examples should be
found, even among her modern imaginative writers, of that degradation of Art
which aims at stirring up rancour and
ill-will against the Jews. Does not ' *Veitel
Itzig*' still cling, like a mark of infamy,
to the memory of even Gustav Freytag?
But unjustifiable and blameworthy as is

* Gesammelte Schriften, iii. 286.

vilifying caricature, it is equally useless and objectionable to exalt and glorify Jewish characters without making evident what is essentially Jewish in them, and without showing the fundamental dependence of their pre-eminent qualities on the historical conditions of their race. It is the duty of an author to introduce his readers into the workshop where his characters are formed, and to allow them to penetrate to the fountain-head of passion and action; the mere epithet "Jewish" tells us nothing, and furnishes no key either to vice or to virtue. How different George Eliot! Led by cordial and loving inclination to the profound study of Jewish national and family life, she has set herself to create *Jewish Characters*, and to recognise and give presentment to the influences which Jewish education is wont to exercise — to prove by TYPES that Judaism is an in-

tellectual and spiritual force, still misap-
prehended and readily overlooked, but
not the less an effective power, for the
future of which it is a good assurance
that it possesses in the body of its adherents a noble, susceptible, and pliant
material which only awaits its final casting
to appear in a glorious form.

An examination of that part of 'Daniel
Deronda' which relates specially to the
Jews and Judaism is inseparable from an
æsthetic estimate of it as a whole. At
a first superficial glance it falls apart
into two entirely unconnected narratives.
Gwendolen Harleth, a brilliant, vivacious,
and haughty girl, gives her hand to Mr
Henleigh Grandcourt, humbled by the im-
poverishment of her family, and dazzled
by the appearance of that perfect man of
the world. But there arises between husband and wife the spectre of a woman,
Lydia Glasher, Grandcourt's cast-off mis-

tress and the mother of his children.
Around Gwendolen are grouped her
mother and the family of her uncle,
Mr Gascoigne, the self-satisfied rector,
whose son, Rex, has been mortally
wounded by the wantonness with which
his wayward cousin has rejected his love.
The theme of this story is the transformation of thoughtlessness and inconstancy
into self-examination and repentance re-
sulting from the ruin of happiness.   Daniel
Deronda, a gifted and noble-hearted youth,
is brought up as a son in the house of Sir
Hugo Mallinger who has no male issue.
He is oppressed by the mystery surround-
ing his birth, concerning which Sir Hugo
keeps him in profound ignorance.   Liber-
ally educated in the fullest sense, he has
of his own impulse acquired powers of self-
direction, determination of will, and independence of judgment.   He saves a poor
desperate girl, Mirah Lapidoth, from sui-

cide, and places her privately in the house
of the mother of his friend, Hans Meyrick,
where she pines restlessly for the mother
and brother whom she has lost. Deronda
discovers the brother — gains access to
the mental life of that wonderful man —
becomes his friend, and the resolute ad-
vancer of his ideas—brings the brother
and sister together, and finally marries
Mirah, after his mother, the singer Alcha-
risi, has declared to him his Jewish origin.
The story closes as he is setting out for
Palestine with his bride to make the ac-
quaintance of a land the political existence
of which it is his mission and his grandest
aim to restore; and we might inscribe it
" A Jewish Tale." Deronda is the centre,
however, of both narratives, for he is the
magnet towards which Gwendolen is mys-
teriously drawn and fixed. But this circumstance would, of itself, scarcely be a
sufficient and satisfactory apology for the

amalgamation by the author of things ir-
relevant. Two lines which cut one another at a common point of intersection
make a mathematical figure, it is true ; but
they cannot form the subject of a work of
art, the unity of which must be preserved
in accordance with fundamental axioms.
For a writer of fiction to couple narratives
which have no essential connection does
not lower his work—it sentences it to
death outright ;. and it is solely because
contemporary criticism has shut its eyes to
the relation of the two stories which run
through ' Daniel Deronda' that its value
as a work of art and its real significance
as a book have not yet received full and
true expression.

As the entire scope of the '*Germania*'
of Tacitus only becomes intelligible to us
after we succeed in picturing to ourselves
the pure Teutonic sunlight which shines
beyond the corrupt Roman society of that

time, so the two narratives which run side by side in 'Daniel Deronda' are to be regarded as pendants mutually illustrating and explaining one another. But it need scarcely be said that the authoress has not fallen into the error of expressly indicating this relation, by crudely holding the two pictures up opposite each other. Her creation belongs to that more earnest kind of art which opens its treasures only to attentive observation, and which rewards us in proportion to the depth of our insight. The contrast afforded by these two narratives is, in truth, an inexhaustible spring of fruitful remark and gratifying perception for the reflective reader. In perusing a work of genius we need not fear that we shall see and find more meaning than it really holds, for it is certain to contain all and more than all that the author was clearly conscious of, while composing it; and it is a light accusation to have read between the lines, for genius has always "*hineingeheimnisst*" more into her creations than appears upon their surface. What was of old said of Holy Writ, holds true of all great imaginative productions—there is a secret as well as an open meaning in them. And in this spirit it is admissible even to give an allegorical interpretation to a work of art.

It would be an exaggeration to say that light and shade have been thrown upon the two sets of circumstances which environ Deronda and Gwendolen, in such a manner that all the light falls upon the former, and all the shade upon the latter; but it cannot be denied that the morality of Deronda's surroundings is greater than that of Gwendolen's, and their vital purport *deeper* and more hearty. Sharper contrasts than Mirah and Gwendolen cannot be conceived. While the one, the Jewess, follows her path in safety through the rudest storms, led as it were by an *innate moral instinct,* in spite of all the cajolements of her wretched father, and in the tender purity of her nature carries an unblemished conscience to meet her coming happiness; the other, groping blindly around and wholly dependent upon aid and assistance from without, staggers and stumbles, and finally lies before us shattered and torn by remorse at the very time when freedom and happiness seem within her reach. The family relations of both are eminently significant. Mirah's whole soul yearns for the mother whom she has lost, and for the brother whom she believes she has lost; and when she is reunited to him, her joy is extreme. Gwendolen has an air of superiority and authoritativeness even towards her careworn mother; and she is in the habit, before her downfall, of regarding her harmless sisters as so many superfluous pieces

of furniture, and treating them as such.
How the hints which are thrown out concerning the wretchedness of the married
life of Mirah's mother throw into dark
relief the conduct of Gwendolen, who actually deliberates whether or not to throw a
rope to her drowning husband, and does
not, as a matter of fact, throw it till too
late! Then compare Henleigh Grandcourt and Daniel Deronda. In the one
we see emptiness and blunted perception,
the disgust which is born of satiety, pol-
ish and fascinating adroitness combined
with absolute want of feeling, and perfect
worldly wisdom hiding heartless barbarity;
in the other, a full and rich mental life, an
open sense for all that is great and beautiful, a moral fibre of the utmost toughness
and yet of the utmost delicacy, and the
readiest and most willing disinterestedness
and self - sacrifice. The one, in a word,
is selfishness incarnate — the other, the

archetype of self-negation. What splendid misery this of Gwendolen's married
life! Her husband she cannot but despise—this man who has already seduced
and betrayed one woman, and by whom
she too, after she becomes his wife, is
maltreated as though she were his dog,
and who regards her as the savage may
regard the jewel which decks his person.
And all this misery must be veiled in
the mantle of social observance, and the
proprieties must be rigidly adhered to.
Everything remains fair outwardly, while
beneath the glitter of the tinsel there is
naught but hollowness and decay, and
while hidden beneath this beauteous en-
velope the heart is lying broken. Contrast
the marriage of Deronda and Mirah, how
happy it is! what a joyous radiance
illumines it! Must we not look upon
Ezra Cohen's humble family even as
thrice blessed in comparison with the

empty prosperity of Sir Hugo Mallinger,
who regards his presumptive heir Grandcourt as a veritable thorn in the flesh,
and vainly seeks to quiet his own inward
discontent by a thousand idle distrac-
tions? The characters seem sometimes to
take voices to themselves, and cry, Compare your superficial splendour, your friv-
olous pleasures, your poor, futile amuse-
ments, your gnawing passions, and your
absorbing vices, with the deep contented-
ness, the all-satisfying delights, and the
moral purity of the higher Jewish life,
and see if these Jews are, after all, so
much more contemptible than yourselves!
What is Gascoigne's son? A victim of
unrequited love, at variance with himself.
In Hans Meyrick, even, there is nothing
but the light temperament of the artist,
for he turns round bitter and hostile upon
Deronda, his best friend and well-wisher,
when the latter's interests come into col-

lision with his own. How shallow, how unsatisfactory, almost mask - like these characters appear, wanting as they are in deep purpose and high yearning, beside Mordecai, that noble flower springing from the dust, that humble Jewish hero! What a people must that be which can produce from its very lowest ranks so pure and lofty a religious genius as Mordecai; and what a system must that be in which a mother's ideal presence is sufficient to keep a daughter modest and dutiful in the very slough of temptation! I am far from imagining that a thinker and poetess of George Eliot's calibre would ever have attempted to represent Judaism as the only source of high-mindedness, and the Jews as the sole and hereditary possessors of all morality. As she herself says, the Caribs regard thieving as a practice peculiarly connected with Christian tenets, because they have chiefly

noticed it among Christians. The specifically Jewish virtues may go along with
the specifically Jewish vices, concerning
which hatred has invented so many fables.
The contrast of the two sets of circumstances is not meant to lead us to one-
sidedness and injustice.   On the contrary,
we ought to learn from it, above all, that
Judaism is no obsolete petrifaction, but a
force beating and pulsating in the hearts
and minds of men—no indifferent shadow
unworthy of our attention, but a fact of
incalculable significance—no object to be
neglected and despised, but a profound
mystery, and a vital challenge to reflection.   Men may think and say, as they
will, that Judaism is the religion of the
past, a piece of road long left behind ; but
it still possesses the power of producing
a Mordecai—it has a *future.*

It has been frivolously asked why the
book is called ' Daniel Deronda,' and not

'Gwendolen Harleth,' or 'Ezra Mordecai Cohen'? We might reply in the old Biblical words, "Thou dost not inquire wisely concerning this," since 'Daniel Deronda' is the hero, the end, and the flower of the whole work. Remembering that the Jewish day begins in the evening, the authoress has chosen to delay her hero's sunrise, and has shown him to us first by the play of moonbeams. The plan of the work is fully justified in representing Gwendolen, viewed as Mirah's counterpart, under all phases of temper, and in revealing to us the most hidden recesses of her wayward and inconstant heart; but it is for Deronda that the development of her character has the deepest meaning. Accurate observation of the orbit which a planet describes throws much light upon the position of the centre of gravity, by which it is attracted and regulated; and we may call Deronda the centre of the path

traced by that wandering-star Gwendolen,
and determined for us by the penetrating
vision of a profound student of the human
heart. From the day when his speaking
glance is first fastened upon her at the
gaming-table of Wiesbaden, his image remains constantly with her. He bursts
upon her life, and awakens her conscience
like a living voice calling her to nobler
things, and to the performance of duty.
He is the only man for whose respect she
has ever craved, gauging as she does, with
a woman's acuteness of perception, his un-
contaminated purity and dignity. No en-
couragement of her weaknesses, no words
of flattery, fall from his grave lips. The
beauty, accustomed to homage and admiration, and whose caprices have seemed
hitherto to rule all the men she has come
in contact with, meets, for the first time, in
Deronda, with a man of self-possession,
whose keen, searching eyes subdue her,

whose good opinion she is forced to acknowledge as valuable, and who summons forth all her powers of self-examination by appearing resolutely to deny her any. He is the magnet which guides and holds her, the anchor to which her fragile bark of life is moored. He becomes an integral part of her conscience, the priest to whom she confesses, and before whom she would fain kneel down—the angel upon whom her upward glances are directed. She has given her hand to a man whom she cannot but despise; she has broken the promise which she gave to his discarded victim, that she would never become his; and she repents in nameless sufferings to which this loathed and detested husband subjects her with an inhuman coolness. One thing alone binds her to life — her guiding-star amid the thunder-clouds and her safety in shipwreck —the memory of Deronda. He is her pro-

tector, her guide, philosopher, and friend—
but her husband he can never be. Poor
psychologists are they who are so little
able to follow the subtle development of
these two characters, as to feel disap-
pointed when they are not united at the
end. For while Gwendolen is the proto-
type of that more harmless form of ego-
tism which loves to fancy that the universe revolves around itself, and which is
sadly disconcerted when that self is at all
roughly handled by fate ; Deronda's whole
being is love and resignation, and he has
been knitted to all that is great too early
to imagine that life contains nothing more
desirable or valuable than his own existence. And although unselfishness may
sometimes succeed in bettering and en-
nobling selfishness, the two are not the
less contradictories, which can never be
entirely reconciled. The meditative reader

will guess for himself how deep a lesson, from a moral and national point of view, is inculcated by the circumstance that Gwendolen and Deronda are not finally made one.

In order to obtain a clear comprehension of Deronda's development, we must divest ourselves of all Philistinism, and break for ever with commonplace hypothesis. Placed from boyhood beyond the reach of care, he early accustoms himself to take an interest in others, and to help and aid them as occasion offers. Courageous in his opinions, and sufficiently independent in mind to examine things for himself, he is free from the cowardice of those circles "where the lack of grave emotion passes for wit," and he neither regards ignorance as ornamental, nor dulness of perception as the necessary accompaniment of the higher education.

In his inexhaustible devotion for others,
it is always he who has been the confidant
receiving innumerable confessions and out-
pourings; he has never had occasion or
opportunity to bestow his own confidence
upon another.   Of the Jews he knows but
little, and feels himself repelled rather
than attracted by them, for it seems to
him that the cultivated among them appear chiefly anxious to affect cosmopol-
itanism; but after rescuing Mirah, he is
led to a closer study of Judaism and its
professors.   We must remember how the
mystery of his origin haunts him, and
further, how he, the benefactor of so
many, has never in his life enjoyed the
boon of unreservedly expressing himself to
a true friend.   In this way we can understand his feelings when, in his search for
Mirah's lost relatives, he comes in contact
with a remarkable Jew, by whom he is entirely captivated.   Gone now is the neglect

with which he has hitherto treated the Jews
—gone now his polite indifference to that
lowly race—for the first *man* whom he
has found worthy of loving reverence and
admiration is a poor, consumptive *Jewish*
watchmaker. And this Jew becomes his
fast friend, and furnishes him with ideas
which impress him for the first time with
a sense of the depth and breadth of life.
He longs that he were a Jew himself, in
order that he might consecrate his days to
the accomplishment of tasks which he now
recognises as noble. *He is a Jew.* His
mother reveals to him, at Genoa, how, in
order to save him from the disgrace at-
taching to his birth, she confided him in
infancy to the care of her admirer Sir
Hugo Mallinger, upon condition of his
being kept in complete ignorance of his
origin. He feels the blood of his forefathers surging within him,—of his grandfather, a Jewish physician in Genoa; and

of his father, the noble Ephraim Charisi,—
for such is his patronymic, Deronda being
merely the name given to him by his
mother.   Mordecai was right,—the fulfilment has taken place.   It is true that he
restrains all violent manifestation of joy
at the news, for he meets his mother as
the Princess Halm-Eberstein, a complete
stranger, as it were, to her own son ; but
there is no need on his part for any expression of triumph, since he was a Jew
at heart long before the tie of kinship
was distinctly made known.   His marriage with Mirah, and the enthusiastic
undertaking of all the tasks and duties
with which his intercourse with Mordecai
has filled his life, form the natural event
toward which the plot is quietly and safely
guided.   It is foolish to ransack an imaginative work for descriptive likenesses of
persons who are to be sought for in life,
or in history, and found, if necessary, in

violation of all probability ; so we need not trouble ourselves to refute the conjectures which have been hazarded concerning the original from which Deronda is drawn. The lover of allegory might with greater justice regard him as typical of mankind in its relations to Judaism, for his story teaches us how the world is beginning to take notice of and admire that system more and more, after having for ages mis-apprehended and neglected it, till some day the discovery will be made that the Jews are flesh of its flesh, and bone of its bone.

If, in drawing Deronda, George Eliot has omitted to bring him near to us as a human being, and has preserved him in a certain stately inaccessibility, on the other hand she has effected a miracle in setting before us a prophet, and in bringing a scarce-ly intelligible and wholly ethereal nature closely home to us. The life which runs

E

in Mordecai's veins is indestructible, and
akin to the spirit with which genius has
animated a Hamlet, a Wallenstein, and a
Faust. If Deronda is the Fulfiller, Mordecai is the Forerunner; if the one is the
Accomplisher, the other is nis John the
Baptist; if the former is the hero, the latter
is the soul of the creation. In the ' Fort-
nightly Review' for April 1866, Mr Lewes,
the husband of the authoress, drew the
character of a Jew in whom some critics
fancy that they have found the original
of Mordecai; and others, again, have been
reminded by the circumstances of his being consumptive and an artisan, of the
spectacle - grinder of the Hague, Baruch
Spinoza, of whom it will never be possible
to deprive the Jews, much as the world
may desire to do so. But although there
may be points both here and there which
recall Mordecai, his character can never be
built up from them, for, carefully and min-

utely finished though he be, he is not so much an artificial piece of workmanship as an intuition sprung, as it were, full grown from the authoress's brain. Mordecai is carved of the wood from which prophets are made, and so far as the supersensuous can be rendered intelligible, it may even be said that in studying him we are introduced into a studio or workshop of the prophetic mind. He is one of the most difficult as well as one of the most successful essays in psychological analysis ever attempted by an author; and in his wonderful portrait, which must be closely studied, and not epitomised or reproduced in extracts, we see glowing enthusiasm united to cabbalistic profundity, and the most morbid tension of the intellectual powers united to clear and well-defined hopes. How has the authoress succeeded in making Mordecai so human and so true to nature? By mixing the gold with an alloy of commoner metal, and by giving the angeiic likeness features which are familiar to us all.

Mordecai, though a Jew, is no hollow enthusiast, and, in spite of all cabbalistic leanings, never loses sight of realities. Tender love for his relatives dwells side by side in his heart with a devoted attachment to his race. When his nearer duty and his lofty schemes clash, he invariably follows the former, as we see, for example, when he renounces his fondest hopes, and straightway breaks off his journey to Palestine, at his hapless mother's cry for help. A strange pair were they from whom Mordecai and his sister sprang. He says of his mother: "She was a mother of whom it might have come to be said, 'Her children arise up and call her blessed.' In her I understand the meaning of that Master who, perceiving the footsteps of his mother, rose up and

said, 'The majesty of the Eternal cometh
near.'" And with regard to their wretched father he comforts his sister with the
words, "Seest thou, our lot is the lot of
Israel? The grief and the glory are
mingled, as the smoke and the flame. It
is because we children have inherited the
good that we feel the evil. These things
are wedded for us, as our father was wedded to our mother." Such a union, not
indeed of actual good and evil, but of
traits apparently contradictory, is revealed
to us in Mordecai's whole being, for we
find in it the divinest flights of imagination
joined to the keenest worldly wisdom, and
the utmost fervour of enthusiasm combined
with the healthiest common-sense. Hence
it is peculiarly characteristic that he cannot conceive the fulfiller of his ideas and
the hero of his race as other than a noble, prosperous, and cultivated man of the
world. When Akiba-ben-Joseph, enrap-

tured at the sight of Bar-Cochba, broke into the words, "A star is arisen in Jacob,"
he may have felt as Mordecai, when
he beheld the realisation of his dreams
and the accomplishment of his yearnings
advance towards him in the person of
Deronda. In deep harmony too with this
entire "frail incorporation of the national consciousness, breathing with difficult
breath," is the circumstance that Mordecai
dies on the eve of setting out for the Holy
Land—that the Sower is not permitted to
behold the ripened fruit, but passes away,
leaving Deronda an actual *testament* to
execute. In the same way the prophets
who presaged in the loftiest visions the
return from the Babylonian Captivity never
set foot on their native soil; and it would
seem indeed that all intellectual and spiritual leaders are destined to share the lot
of Moses, who could only gaze from afar
upon the land which was to crown his

labours and complete the mission of his life.

The marvellous versatility of our authoress, whose brush paints with equal readiness the miniature life of childhood and the most stormy and eventful pictures of passion, is further revealed by her presenting us with the modest and fragrant floweret Mirah, between two such striking growths as Deronda and Mordecai; and the affection which the pair bear for her amid all their imperious longings and stirring ideas affects us as a soft, soothing note heard among resounding chords. Only a master - hand could have succeeded in sketching and finishing her figure on the canvas. The account which she gives her protectress, Mrs Meyrick, in plain, affecting language which reminds us of the Bible, of the wandering life she led with her weak degraded father, of the moral power of her mother's memory, and of the irresistible strength with which her love for race and faith kept ever growing in her heart, is of itself valuable testimony to the frequently unconscious influence which Judaism still exercises upon the feelings and sentiments of its professors. Before the pregnant brevity and depth of feeling with which the winning Jewish maiden tells her tale, prejudices are scattered like the clouds; and proselytism must be silent when it sees with what gentle fervour she cherishes and clings to Judaism in her heart of hearts. Zunz has said that in that faith we have a plastic representation of family love; and we seem to see this the most clearly where, as here, filial and sisterly affection find embodiment in an admirable example of human nature. And this disposition is preserved intact among the rude billows of experience, and brings the poor girl unhurt through trials which at one time drive her to the very verge of suicide. In her depth and fervour the little Jewess strikes us as a being from another world beside the emptiness and stupidity which characterise so many of her cultivated and acccmplished companions. When was the gratitude of a girlish heart more sweetly depicted than in Mirah Cohen—or Lapidoth, as her father calls her? She is unable to understand how she can be anything to Deronda, and the jealousy which Gwendolen's passionate clinging to him arouses in her is timid and half unconscious. With the love of truth which distinguishes genius, George Eliot has fearlessly dared to accuse English society of scarcely comprehending a phenomenon such as Mirah, so modest and tender, in spite of her having been on the stage, and in whom there is no trace of that "Jewish impudence," so confidently expected in women of her race.

But the colours in 'Daniel Deronda'

have not been laid on with one-sided preference or blind partiality ; and the meaning and truth of the authoress's types become all the clearer when we notice the justice with which shadows both deep and light are brought out in this picture of the Jewish people. The little incidental strokes, for instance, by means of which she gives us an insight into the narrowness of the circumstances of Ezra Cohen and his family, and their calculating, business-like mode of expressing kind feeling, are of inimitable grace. George Eliot's satire has none of the bitterness of hatred, but springs, like all true humour, from love ; and for this reason the pictures which she has drawn of the Jews are of far greater force than the caricaturing misrepresentations which an active hatred hawks about the world. He has been at all times the true poet who could find the rift of blue mirrored in the ditch, and

see a trace of the Divine in the most abject
of mankind.   Thus in placing Mordecai
in the family of the pawnbroker Cohen,
for whom she certainly has no great affection or esteem, the authoress has paid
a gracious tribute of recognition to the
Jewish race.   He is no relation, but only
a namesake of Ezra Cohen, who has taken
him into his house "as a compound of
workman, dominie, vessel of charity, inspired idiot, man of piety, and (if he were
inquired into) dangerous heretic."   It is
amusing to read how Ezra, as it were, ex-
cuses himself to Deronda for his weak-
ness in retaining so superfluous a member
in his household.   Gwendolen Harleth
says, in her prosperity, that she does not
like poor children.   We see that benev-
olence to the poor is a necessity for the
family of the humble Jewish pawnbroker.
Particularly happy is the authoress's way
of hitting off the peculiarity common to

so many Jews of being unwilling to dis-
cuss the forms and ceremonials of their
religion in the presence of Christians.
When Mordecai, at the desire of Deronda,
quits his old abode and prepares to set
up house along with his sister Mirah, the
grandmother of little Jacob Cohen—who
is, by the way, a great favourite with the
authoress—remarks, "'Well, I hope there'll
be nothing in the way of your getting
kosher meat, Mordecai.' 'That's all right,
that's all right,' replied Cohen, as if anxious
to cut off inquiry on matters in which he
was uncertain of the guest's [Deronda's]
position." While all the world is satisfied
that avarice is congenital among the Jews,
and their special inheritance rather than
the inheritance of all mankind, George
Eliot expresses a very different opinion.
She says of Ezra Cohen: "He was
not clad in the sublime pathos of the
martyr, and his taste for money-getting

seemed to be *favoured with that success* which has been the most exasperating difference in the greed of the Jews during all ages of their dispersion." To be greedy, then, is human; it is successful greed that seems to be peculiarly Jewish. Mordecai's language with regard to the Cohens is remarkable: "'The Cohens seem to have an affection for you,' said Deronda. 'And I for them,' was the immediate answer. 'They have the heart of the Israelite within them, though they are as the horse and the mule, without understanding beyond the narrow path they tread.'" To the question, "Is there any kinship between this family and yours?" he replies, "Only the kinship of Israel. My soul clings to these people, who have sheltered me and given me succour out of the affection that abides in Jewish hearts, as a sweet odour in things long crushed and hidden from the outer air." There

is a fine touch of humour, too, in the name
of the musical genius of the book, the critic
and judge of Gwendolen and Mirah.   He
is unmistakably a Jew, but he never be-
trays himself, although the unfortunate
name Julius Klesmer is enough for the
initiated, and causes Mrs Arrowpoint even
to take the first opportunity of breaking
out into references to Jews and gypsies
when the question of her daughter's marriage to the artist comes on the *tapis*.
What an insight into land and people these
bitter words reveal which the authoress
puts in the mouth of that splendid figure
Joseph Kalonymos, the Jew of Mayence
—"We increase our strength in safety,
and *the learning of all Germany is fed
and fattened by Jewish brains — though
they keep not always their Jewish hearts*"!
Who can deny this?   The hit goes right
into the gold!

Poetical justice in 'Daniel Deronda'

finds its account in the care which the authoress takes to blend a degree of shade with the light which streams forth like a halo from Deronda and Mordecai. It is always painful to hear fair lips pronouncing ugly words, and we are wounded and annoyed by the hard and rugged language of Deronda's mother, the daughter of the Genoese physician, Daniel Charisi. Masculine in her ideas, this woman has always regarded Judaism with all its rules and formalities as an oppressive burden; but her stern father was resolutely opposed to all her loose artistic inclinations, and forced her to marry the man of his choice. When her father and husband are both dead, she determines to break all family ties, and gives her infant son to her admirer, Sir Hugo Mallinger, in order that the boy may be spared all those troubles and sorrows which embittered her own young days, and were the ruin, indeed, of

her life. But the ghost of her father arises
in her soul and calls upon her to restore
the child to the race from whom he has
been taken ; and she has to confess to that
child, in after-years, the evil deed she did
him.   Her life as we see it is a broken
existence—a picture of apostasy punished,
and of treachery betrayed.   If any further
evidence were wanting to clear the authoress from the imputation of a blind partiality for the Jews, we should find it in her
sketch of old Lapidoth, who is a rascal fit
to grace any museum of human depravity,
and who is drawn with such truth and
reality that we forget in looking at him
that he is a mere creation of the fancy.
But no Jew will find it unnatural that this
wretched creature can call Mordecai and
Mirah his children, for it is notorious that
in Jewish families it is generally owing to
the mother that children are prevented
from following in the footsteps of their

fathers. Thus even the very lowest and most degraded persons in the work we are considering are stamped with a peculiar Jewish impress, and the circumstance that they are Jews is not without significance for their destinies and characters.

Leader of the present so-called realistic school, our authoress keeps up in this work the reputation she has won of possessing the most minute knowledge of the subjects she handles, by the manner in which she has described the Jews—the Great Unknown of humanity. She has penetrated into their history and literature affectionately and thoroughly; and her knowledge in a field where ignorance is still venial if not expressly authorised, has astonished even experts. In her selection of almost always unfamiliar quotations, she shows a taste and a facility of reference really amazing. When shall we see a German writer exhibiting the

F

courteous kindliness of George Eliot, who
makes Deronda study Zunz's ' *Synagogale
Poesie,*' and places the monumental words
which open his chapter entitled " *Leiden* "
at the head of the passage in which she
introduces us to Ezra Cohen's family, and
to the Club-meeting at which Mordecai
gives utterance to his ideas concerning the
future of Israel ? She is as familiar with
the views of Jehuda-ha-Levi as with the
dreams and longings of the Cabbalists, and
as conversant with the splendid names of
our Hispano-Arabian epoch as with the
moral aphorisms of the Talmud and the
subtle meaning contained in Jewish le-
gends. Here is an instance : " There is a
legend told of the Emperor Domitian, that
having heard of a Jewish family of the
house of David, whence the ruler of the
world was to spring, he sent for its members in alarm, but quickly released them
on observing that they had the hands of

work-people—being of just the opposite
opinion with that Rabbi who stood wait-
ing at the gate of Rome in confidence
that the Messiah would be found among
the destitute who entered there." It is
by the piety and tenderness with which
she treats Jewish customs that the authoress shows how supreme her cultivation
and refinement are; and the small number of mistakes* which can be detected

* One such mistake—unless, indeed, the authoress
has had the Sephardic custom in her eye — is to be
found in the intimation that Deronda saw the *Talith*
worn on the Friday evening in the Frankfort Synagogue
and at Genoa. The "thanksgiving which was carried
on by responses" (Book IV., 362) cannot mean the
Mesuman, for little Jacob could not have taken part
in that. Ezra Cohen's assertion (Book VI., 322) that
the Jews thank God every Sabbath that they were not
made women needs correction also, since this benedic-
tion is in daily use. "*Babli*," again, cannot be called
an "affectionate sounding diminutive" (Book VIII.,
238), for in that case we should have to apply that term
to "Talmud babli" also, for which the single word
stands. Nor is it permissible to speak of the "vast vol-
ume of the Babylonian Talmud" (ibid.), since the Talmud
actually fills twelve volumes.

in her descriptions of Jewish life and ritual may put to the blush even writers who belong to that race.   What a loving insight into the spirit of Judaism is expressed by this reflection evoked by the confession of unity in the Shemah : " The divine unity embraced as its consequence the ultimate unity of mankind.   The nation which has been scoffed at for its separateness, has given a binding theory to the human race."

There is no delusion on George Eliot's part that the ideas and characters which she has given to the world in this work will be received with unanimity in Christian circles, or with pleasure by all Jews. She knows as well as any one the objections which may be urged against her leading idea ; and Mordecai has to endure some very hard hits at his holy enthusiasm in the Philosopher's Club at the " Hand and Banner."   Gideon, the Jewish optician,

calls out to him, "As to the connection
of our race with Palestine, it has been
perverted by superstition till it's as de-
moralising as the old poor-law. The raff
and scum go there to be maintained like
able-bodied paupers, and to be taken special
care of by the angel Gabriel when they
die. It's no use fighting against facts, we
must look where they point; that is what
I call rationality. The most learned and
liberal among us who are attached to our
religion are for clearing our liturgy of all
such notions as a literal fulfilment of the
prophecies about restoration, and so on.
Prune it of a few useless rites and literal
interpretations of that sort, and our religion is the simplest of all religions, and
makes no barrier, but a union, between
us and the rest of the world." Others
will say that the establishment of a national State is not the aim of Jewish history at all. Taking the analogy of the

plants which undergo their various stages
of growth, development, and flower, to the
sole end that their seeds may be produced,
this class regards the State as a mere
vessel in which peculiar and characteristic
national ideas are produced and perfected.
And when the vessel is broken, its contents
are forced out and serve to fructify the
earth. Greece has been broken in this
way, but she still works on, and will work
indestructibly for ever, as the vital teacher
of all beauty. Rome, the earthen Colossus,
has fallen asunder into potsherds, but the
system of jurisprudence which the Romans
brought to maturity forms the basis of jurisprudence in every quarter of the world.
And now the time of fulfilment has come
for Judæa; her political form has indeed
been swept from the surface of the earth,
but her children have spread themselves
abroad among the nations as teachers,
bringing the ineradicable seeds of eternal

truth to the heathen, and as messengers
coming upon an errand from on high. In
the very circumstance of their dispersion
may lie Fulfilment, for Israel will be greatest when she labours under every zone. So
some would argue; but these objections do
not touch the value of 'Daniel Deronda'
as a work of art; and, strictly speaking,
not even the ideas of which it is the mouth-
piece. For the establishment of a Jewish
national centre will not prevent the race
from disseminating itself among the other
nations of the globe. On the contrary, the
influence of the Jews who remain scattered
will be strengthened and supported by the
consciousness which they will then possess
that they are members of a united and
recognised community. George Eliot is
one of those who believe that Judaism is
not only a religion, but a nationality also,
and that this has a voice which cries out
even in those who have apparently sepa-

rated themselves from their people of their own free will, and in those who have been stolen from their race by their parents. The thoughts which lie slumbering in Deronda are brought to consciousness by Mordecai, and the explanations which he receives from his mother fix them firmly in his mind as realities. His own words express this most clearly when he says to Mordecai : " It is you who have given shape to what, I believe, was an inherited yearning—the effect of brooding, passionate thoughts in many ancestors— thoughts that seem to have been intensely present in my grandfather. Suppose the stolen offspring of some mountain tribe brought up in a city of the plain, or one with an inherited genius for painting and born blind—the ancestral life would be within them as a dim longing for unknown objects and sensations, and the spell-bound habit of their inherited frames would be like a cunningly-wrought musical instrument, never played on, but quivering throughout in uneasy, mysterious moanings of its intricate structure that, under the right touch, gives music. Something like that, I think, has been my experience. Since I began to read and know, I have always longed for some ideal task, in which I might feel myself the heart and brain of a multitude—some social captainship, which would come to me as a duty, and not be striven for as a personal prize. You have raised the image of such a task for me—*to bind our race together in spite of heresy.*"

But in whatever way these questions may be decided, the book remains untouched as a work of art. In judging an imaginative work, it is not the critic's business to determine whether or not its ideas be true, but solely to examine whether these ideas have permeated the

flesh and blood of the characters, and
made them lifelike, and able to captivate
and carry us along with them. And it is
not till we have taken up this point of
view that the conclusion will force itself
upon us that 'Daniel Deronda' is a Jewish book not only in the sense that it
treats of Jews, but also in the sense that
it is pre-eminently fitted for being under-
stood and appreciated by Jews; indeed,
they only are qualified to embrace and
enjoy its full significance. For what is it
that binds us to the poet? What else
than his power of expressing the words
which rise to all our lips and yet remain
unuttered, of giving voice to the feelings
of each of us, of weeping with one and
making merry with another, and of having
something to offer to every human heart
which may often have been sighed for, but
which has never been realised and grasped
so securely hitherto. Naturally it is a

Jewish heart alone that can feel the entire magic of a creation woven from the
highest hopes of that nation's soul. The
book will win friends among the Jews,
not only through the feeling of pride
which may well arise in the breast of every
honest man who sees his people honoured,
but also, and chiefly, through the profound
satisfaction which it will afford the thinker
to find his individuality recognised and
explained by a stranger. The one will
rejoice heartily at finding what he long
ago implicitly discerned, here so definitely
expressed; and the eyes of the other will
grow dim with tears when he beholds the
dear, regretted features of a well-known
face greeting him from the framework of
the tale.

Loud has been the weeping and terrible
the gnashing of teeth in the camp of the
critics. Of what has the revered and idol-
ised Queen of novelists been thinking that

she should descend to the Jews ?   George
Eliot has experienced personally what
the world's hatred of that race amounts
to, and that she has done so affords the
strongest proof of the moral tendency
which lies in her inimitable performance.
It is not only the Jew of flesh and blood
whom men encounter every day upon the
streets that they hate, but the Jew under
whatever shape he may appear ; and even
the airy productions of the poet's fancy
are denounced when they venture to take
that people as their subject.   The majority of readers regard the world to which
they are introduced in 'Daniel Deronda'
as one foreign, strange, and repulsive.
Our authoress — whom it has hitherto
been the custom to extol to the skies,
and to whom the critics have, up to this
time, been related more as partisans than
as judges — has been abandoned on this
occasion by almost the entire body, not

one of whom has been able to make up his mind to do homage to a genius which has lost its way in the lowly walks of Jewish life. Indignation and perplexity will doubtless some day vanish, however, and give place to joy, when it is recognised that the literature of the world has been enriched by a work worthy to be crowned and garlanded as a public defence of the right of private judgment against the attacks of prejudice and falsehood.

George Eliot has not thrown herself away upon an unworthy object. It is a beautiful characteristic of Judaism that it cherishes the memory of its alien benefactors in imperishable remembrance and everlasting honour. It is a hundred years since Lessing heralded in his 'Nathan' the dawn of a new epoch for the race, and from 'Nathan' to 'Deronda' the world has not stood still; the most unlooked-for

events have taken place, and the self-consciousness of Judaism has itself undergone
a change.   In ' Nathan' we see a man who
comes forward for the vindication of his
rights as a human being, and he may be
regarded as giving expression to an ab-
stract religious idea rather than to historical and organic Judaism ; it is the end of
all wisdom in his eyes that the right ring
is lost, and that his peculiar teachings have
no greater claim to authenticity and trust-
worthiness than those of another.   How
different in ' Deronda' !   Here the Jew
demands the rights pertaining to his race,
and claims admittance into the community
of nations as a legitimate member.   The
blood of the prophets surges in his veins,
the voice of God calls to him, and he becomes conscious and emphatically declares
that he is not as others are ; the days of
levelling are over.   Contrasted with the
revolting treatment to which public opin-

ion still subjects Judaism, its glorious ex-
altation in ' Deronda ' is most healthy and
beneficial. Where calumny and obtuse-
ness see nothing but *disjecta membra*, the
prophetic eye of the poetess perceives a
complete and perfect body destined to a
renewed life of fresh and manly vigour.
The march of universal history has veri-
fied Lessing's predictions, and when another century shall have passed away,
time will show what genius has to say
of Deronda's grandchildren. But this is
certain in the meantime—As *Gotthold
Ephraim Lessing* has endeared himself
for ever to the hearts of the Jewish race,
so, too, will it always be gratefully declared that *George Eliot has deserved right
well of Judaism.*

Printed in the United States
101566LV00008B/423/A